LET'S LEARN
FRENCH

Written and edited by
Nicola Wright, Carol Watson and Philippa Moyle

Illustrated by
Kim Woolley and Teresa Foster

zigzag

Contents

This book was created by
Zigzag Publishing Ltd, The Barn,
Randolph's Farm, Brighton Road,
Hurstpierpoint, West Sussex BN6 9EL

Designers: Teresa Foster, Jane Felstead,
 Suzi Hooper, Jenny Searle and
 Jonathan Skelton
Design Manager: Kate Buxton
Additional illustrations: Guy Smith
Consultants: Claire Nozières and
 Katherine Folliot
Pronunciation guide: Philippa Tomlinson
 and Kay Barnham
Series concept: Tony Potter

This edition published 1994
by Zigzag Publishing Ltd

Copyright © Zigzag Publishing Ltd 1993 first editions
Copyright © Zigzag Publishing Ltd 1994 revised edition

ISBN 1-85993 049 2

Colour separations by RCS Graphics Ltd, Leeds
Printed by New Interlitho, Italy

About this book

In this book you can find out all about France, French people and the French language. Discover what the French like to eat and drink, what they do for a living and what famous French places look like.

Where France is in the world

North America

Europe

Asia

South America

Africa

Australia

Find out what French children do in their spare time and how they celebrate French festivals.

Hello!

Bonjour!

You will meet the Flaubert family and see what they say in lots of situations. They show you how to say the French words. You will find many useful French words and phrases throughout this book to help you increase your French vocabulary.

From page 26 onwards, you can learn how to speak French.

Map of France

France is one of the largest countries in Europe. It is bordered by eight other countries: Spain, Andorra, Monaco, Switzerland, Luxembourg, Germany, Belgium and Italy. Even so, almost half of France's border is coastline.

Longest river:
The Loire, 1,020 km. Many beautiful châteaux line its banks.

le fleuve
river

Corsica

France owns the island of Corsica. It lies in the Mediterranean Sea, 170 km south of France.

The French landscape varies greatly. In some places there are high mountains and thick forests. In others there are rolling fields and sandy beaches.

la carte
map

English Channel

Cherbourg

Le H

Caen

Normandy

Brest

St-Malo

Brittany

Rennes

Le

Loire Valley

Loire

Nantes

Ce

Poitou-Cha

Lim

Bordeaux

Dor

Garon

Aquitaine

Mid
Pyrén

Pyrenees

Spain

Belgium

Luxembourg

Germany

Switzerland

Italy

Monaco

Andorra

Paris

Lille

Amiens

Orléans

Metz

Strasbourg

Dijon

Besançon

Clermont-Ferrand

St-Etienne

Lyon

Grenoble

Montpellier

Marseille

Toulon

St-Tropez

Cannes

Nice

Nord-Pas-de-Calais

Picardy

-de-France

Champagne

Lorraine

Alsace

Franche-Comté

Burgundy

Jura Mountains

Savoie

Mont Blanc

Alps

Auvergne

Massif Central

Rhône Valley

Rhône

Cévennes

Provence

Côte d'Azur

anguedoc-
oussillon

Mediterranean Sea

Seine

Key

★ Capital city

♜ Major town

🪣 Seaside resort

🚢 Port

Scale

0   50   100   150

kilometres

Highest mountain:
Mont Blanc, Alps,
4,807 metres.
It is the highest
mountain in
western Europe.

la montagne
mountain

5

Facts about France

Although France is twice as large as the United Kingdom, about the same number of people live there, so it is much less crowded.

Size:
543,965 sq km

Population:
56,647,000

This has been the French flag since the French Revolution in 1789. It is called the 'tricolore' which means a flag with three stripes.

le drapeau
flag

The Head of State is the President, who is elected every seven years by the French people.

Language

Although the official language is French, there are other languages spoken in parts of the country:

la langue
language

Breton is spoken in the north-west. It is related to Cornish, Welsh and Irish.

Basque is spoken in the region around the Spanish border. It is unlike any other European language.

A dialect of German is spoken in Alsace and Lorraine. These areas used to belong to Germany.

6

Money

French money is divided into francs (F) and centimes (ct). 100 centimes equal 1 franc.

l'argent
money

Banknotes are issued for the following amounts: 500, 200, 100, 50 and 20 francs. The heads of famous French people appear on the notes.

There are 10, 5, 2, 1 and ½ franc coins, and 20, 10 and 5 centime coins.

la pièce de monnaie
coin

le billet de banque
banknote

Capital city:
Paris

Official name:
La République Française
(French Republic)

Some things France is well known for

les voitures
cars
Renault, Citroën, Peugeot

les avions
aircraft
Concorde

le parfum
perfume
Chanel, Dior, Givenchy

le fromage
cheese
Camembert, Brie and about 400 other varieties

le vin
wine
Champagne, Burgundy, Bordeaux and many others

Regions of France

France is divided into many different regions, and includes the island of Corsica in the Mediterranean. The scenery, weather and way of life vary greatly from region to region.

The north of France has cold winters, warm summers, and plenty of rainfall.

le temps
weather

le nord
north

le sud
south

In the south of France it is hot and dry in the summer and mild and moist in the winter.

Many of the seaside resorts along the south coast, such as Cannes and Nice, were once small fishing ports. Now they are holiday places for rich, fashionable people from all over Europe.

le ski nautique
waterskiing

The French call the south coast the 'Côte d'Azur', which means 'sky-blue coast', because of its good weather.

About one-fifth of France is covered with woodland. In the Vosges and Jura mountains in the east there are large pine and fir forests.

la forêt
forest

Wild animals, including boar, foxes, beavers and chamois (a kind of antelope) can be found in these regions.

In the east, the high mountains of the Alps are covered with snow all year and the scenery is spectacular.

le ski
skiing

This region is very popular for skiing in the winter and hiking in summer.

la neige
snow

Normandy, in the north, has a flat coastline with long sandy beaches.

la côte
coast

la plage
beach

The coastline of Brittany in the north-west is rocky with many inlets.

Several large rivers run through the high, flat land of central France. Beautiful countryside and picturesque towns line their banks.

There are vineyards all over France. Most regions produce their own wine. Champagne and Burgundy are some of the best known.

le raisin
grapes

le vignoble
vineyard

Paris

Paris is the largest and most important French city. It is the capital of the country and the centre of industry, business, fashion and entertainment.

The original city was built on an island in the middle of the River Seine. The island became known as the Ile de la Cité (City Island). During the 12th century, the beautiful Notre-Dame cathedral was built on it.

Notre-Dame Cathedral

Paris is famous for its arts. There are many street painters in the district called Montmartre. Famous artists like Renoir and Picasso once lived there.

l'artiste
artist

The quickest and cheapest way to get around the city is on the Métro underground railway.

Over 9,000,000 people live in Paris and its suburbs, which is almost one-fifth of the total French population.

les gens
people

RATP

Famous places

Palais du Louvre and the glass pyramids (art gallery)

Sacré-Cœur (a church on top of the hill of Montmartre with splendid views of Paris)

Arche de la Défense (built to mark 200 years since the French Revolution)

Arc de Triomphe (the Tomb of the Unknown Soldier is under it)

Panthéon (church containing the tombs of some of those people who died during the Revolution)

Eiffel Tower (built in 1889 for an exhibition)

Place de la Concorde (many people were guillotined here during the Revolution)

Pompidou Centre (modern exhibition halls)

Moulin Rouge (one of the most famous nightclubs in Paris)

In a typical French town

There is a square in the middle of most French towns and villages. All the main shops are grouped around it. Often there is a statue or water fountain in the centre.

la boulangerie
baker's

le magasin
shop

le tabac
tobacconist

People gather to talk in the main square under the shade of trees.

la charcuterie
pork butcher's

le supermarché
supermarket

Les agents de police work in the towns.
Les gendarmes work in the country.
Both types of police wear a blue uniform.

la poste
post office

l'épicerie-alimentation
grocer's

la librairie-papeterie-maison de la presse
bookshop-stationers-newspaper shop

l'hôtel de ville
town hall

l'église
church

There are lots of churches in France. Most people are Roman Catholic.

la banque
bank

la pharmacie
chemist's

la droguerie
hardware store

la pâtisserie-confiserie
cake and sweet shop

le boucherie
butcher's

Boules (bowls) is a popular traditional game. A small metal ball is thrown on the ground. Each person throws a larger metal ball so that it lands as near to the little one as possible. Points are scored for landing nearest to the small ball.

la boutique de vêtements
clothes shop

le syndicat d'initiative
tourist information

13

Eating in France

The French are famous for their love of food and cooking. Meals are never rushed and French restaurants are some of the best in the world.

Here is a typical French breakfast (le petit déjeuner) called a continental breakfast:

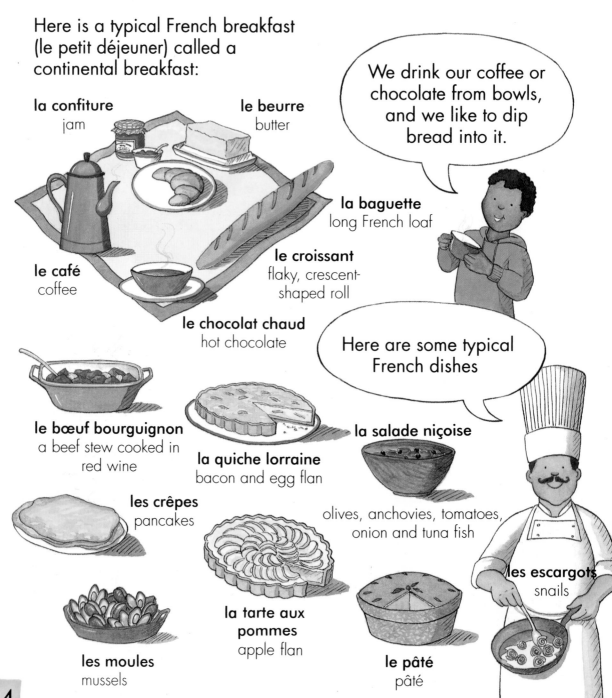

la confiture
jam

le beurre
butter

We drink our coffee or chocolate from bowls, and we like to dip bread into it.

la baguette
long French loaf

le café
coffee

le croissant
flaky, crescent-shaped roll

le chocolat chaud
hot chocolate

Here are some typical French dishes

le bœuf bourguignon
a beef stew cooked in red wine

la quiche lorraine
bacon and egg flan

la salade niçoise

olives, anchovies, tomatoes, onion and tuna fish

les crêpes
pancakes

les escargots
snails

la tarte aux pommes
apple flan

les moules
mussels

le pâté
pâté

Some well-known French drinks

l'apéritif
apéritif
Pernod, Ricard

le vin
wine
Champagne, Burgundy, Muscadet

la bière
beer
usually made in Alsace

le cidre
cider

made in Normandy and Brittany

l'eau minérale
mineral water
Evian (still), Perrier (fizzy)

la liqueur
liqueur
Kirsch, Chartreuse

A French meal

Lunch (le déjeuner) and dinner (le dîner) are usually large meals and can go on for hours.

le repas
meal

The meal starts with soup or crudités (raw salad or vegetables). Next there is a meat or fish course. The vegetables are often eaten after this.

The meal ends with cheese, followed by a pudding or fruit.

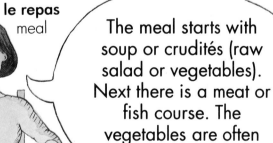

What people do

France is a large country, and people live and work differently in the various regions. Some people work in busy industrial areas. Others live in the countryside and are farmers.

France is an important farming country, but today machines do much of the work. Fewer people now work on the land than in industry.

Farmers grow cereals (wheat, oats and barley), grapes, fruit and vegetables. Dairy farmers produce cheese, butter, milk, cream and yoghurt.

le fermier
farmer

French railways employ many people. France's Train à Grande Vitesse (TGV) runs between towns all over the country and holds the world rail speed record.

Lait

Sheep farming is common in the south-east and the central plateau. Roquefort cheese is made from sheep's milk.

France is especially famous for its wine. The wine business employs many people, especially in the grape-picking season. The wines and brandies of France are sold all over the world.

le mouton
sheep

Steel, cars, shipbuilding, aircraft, textiles, perfume and food products are some of France's main industries.

l'usine
factory

French farms and fisheries produce almost all the food the people need.

The people of Brittany (called Bretons) are mainly farmers and fishermen. Nearly a half of the fish caught in the sea around France come from this region.

le pêcheur
fisherman

Figs, oranges, lemons, almonds and olives are grown in the south, along the Mediterranean coast. Flowers are grown there, too, for making perfume. The perfume business is very important.

Many French people work in hotels and restaurants. There is an important tourist trade, especially in the Alps and along the Mediterranean coast.

Brasserie

Le Bistro

Children in France

Here you can find out something about school life in France, and about how French children spend their time.

l'école
school

les vacances
holidays

The school day usually begins at 8.30 in the morning and lasts until 4.00 in the afternoon. There may be classes on Saturday mornings, but Wednesdays are normally free.

School children have quite long holidays. They get: one week at Toussaint (All Saints) which is the autumn half-term; two weeks at Christmas; two weeks at the end of February (winter half-term); two weeks at Easter, and two months in the summer.

les devoirs
homework

At most French schools, children do not wear a uniform. Many of them wear jeans, a sweatshirt and trainers.

les vêtements
clothes

Though French children have long holidays, many of them have to do 'devoirs de vacances' (holiday homework), revising what they have learned at school during the year.

18

Many schools also offer what they call 'classe de neige' (class in the snow) or 'classe de mer' (class by the sea). The whole class spends a week in a ski resort or at the seaside. Lessons go on as usual, but the children also do outdoor activities.

All children take part in sports at school.

le sport
sport

Athletics, gymnastics and team sports such as football, volley ball and basketball are played.

le skateboard
skateboarding

As in many other countries, there are crazes. Over recent years these have included skateboarding and electronic games.

One of the favourite pastimes of many French children is reading comics. Characters such as Asterix and Tintin are very popular.

la bande dessinée
comic

19

History of France

58 BC

The Romans, led by Julius Caesar, invaded France (or Gaul, as it was then called). It remained part of the huge Roman Empire for 400 years.

1066

le roi
king

William the Conqueror (from Normandy, in northern France) invaded England, won the Battle of Hastings, and was crowned king of England.

1337-1453

During the Hundred Years War, England invaded France. The English won parts of France, but Joan of Arc inspired the French to rise up against them. She was captured by the English and burned to death in 1431. By 1453 the English had been defeated.

1789

In 1789 the French people decided to overthrow the king and nobles so the people themselves could rule the country. King Louis XVI, and many others, were beheaded. This was called the French Revolution.

le soldat
soldier

'Liberty leading the people'
– a painting by Delacroix

1830 - 1848

1804

Napoleon Bonaparte was a brilliant soldier, who became the people's hero during the French Revolution. He crowned himself Emperor in 1804. He was defeated by the English at the Battle of Waterloo in 1815.

After the Battle of Waterloo, the French royal family and nobles tried to return to power. However, they were defeated by the people in two more revolutions in 1830 and 1848.

1919

During World War II (1939-1945), Hitler's troops invaded France. General Charles de Gaulle led the French Resistance fighters who worked to defeat the Germans. France was eventually freed in 1944.

1944

France lost the regions of Alsace and Lorraine to Germany during the Franco-Prussian War in 1870. However, at the Treaty of Versailles at the end of World War I (1914-1918), Germany gave them back to France.

1958

In 1958 France joined with West Germany, Italy, Belgium, the Netherlands and Luxembourg to form the European Economic Community.

Famous places

Thousands of tourists from all over the world visit France every year. There are many beautiful and interesting places to see. Here are some of them.

Near Paris is the enormous and magnificent royal palace called the Château de Versailles, built 300 years ago for King Louis XIV.

le pique-nique
picnic

Visitors picnic beside the many lakes, fountains and statues in the grounds.

Mont-Saint-Michel was built as a monastery on a tiny island off the coast of Normandy. When the tide is low, you can walk or drive to it across the sand.

l'île
island

Annecy is a beautiful old lake-side town in the Savoie region. Visitors like to go boating on the lake.

le lac
lake

le pont
bridge

The Pont du Gard is a huge aqueduct in Provence, built over 2,000 years ago by the Romans. It carried spring water 35 km into the town of Nîmes.

The old town of Rouen in Normandy has an important place in French history. It was here that Joan of Arc was burned to death by the English for leading the French against them. A monument marks where she was burned.

Jeanne d'Arc
Joan of Arc

The Château de Chambord, in the Loire Valley, is one of France's most extravagant châteaux. It has 440 rooms and a maze of staircases and turrets.

Corsica, a lovely island in the Mediterranean Sea, is a popular place for holidays. You can enjoy deep-sea diving in the clear, warm water.

la plage
beach

Festivals

The French love celebrations. Many festivals are held throughout the year. Some celebrate religious occasions and historical events, others the arts. Some regions have their own festivals.

On 14 July, everyone in France celebrates the storming of the Bastille prison at the beginning of the French Revolution. There are torchlit processions, military parades and firework displays. People decorate their houses with flags and dance in the streets all night.

la fête
festival

le festival du film
film festival

There are many festivals celebrating the arts, including theatre, cinema, dance and music. The International Film Festival, held in Cannes every year, attracts famous stars and film-makers who come to see the year's new films.

In some parts of northern France, huge models of local historical heroes, called Les Géants (the giants) are paraded through the streets during special festivals.

At Christmas, people ski down the mountains at night carrying flaming torches.

le géant
giant

In the big wine-producing areas, local people celebrate the end of the grape harvest every autumn.

They hold dances and taste the new wine. Members of the wine societies dress up in traditional costumes.

le cyclisme
cycling

The Tour de France is a cycle race that is held each summer. Cyclists from all over the world take part. Millions watch the race, either along the route or on television.

l'âne
donkey

On 6 December, people in the north and east celebrate the Festival of St Nicolas (Father Christmas), the patron saint of children. In many towns a man dressed as St Nicolas walks through the streets with a donkey, handing out sweets to children.

On 6 January the French celebrate la Fête des Rois (festival of the three kings). People eat a special cake, and whoever finds the bean hidden in it is King or Queen of the Day.

A huge carnival is held in Nice to celebrate Mardi Gras (Shrove Tuesday). For 12 days people watch the processions of colourful floats and people in fancy dress.

You can join in a battle of flowers with the people on floats.

le char
float

le cortège
procession

25

How to speak French

**Now you can find out how to speak French.
The Flaubert family show you what to say in many different
situations. Here they are to introduce themselves.**

The Flaubert family

Nous nous appelons Monsieur et Madame Flaubert.
(Noo noo zapperlong Mersyer ay Madam Flowbair.)
We are Monsieur and Madame Flaubert.

Je m'appelle Marie.
(Jer mappell Marie.)
My name is Marie.

Je m'appelle Jean.
(Jer mappell Jong.)
My name is Jean.

**Everything the Flaubert family says is written in French
and English. There is also a guide to help you pronounce
the French words.**

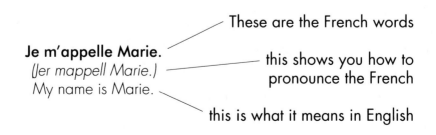

Je m'appelle Marie. — These are the French words
(Jer mappell Marie.) — this shows you how to
pronounce the French
My name is Marie. — this is what it means in English

How to say French words

The pronunciation guide shows you how to say the French words. These notes will help you to use the guide:

- When you see the letters 'ew', purse your lips as if you are going to make an 'oo' sound, but say 'ee' instead.
- The letters 'er' are pronounced like the 'er' in under.

- You should say the letters 'ng' very quickly, so that the 'g' is almost silent. It should sound like the 'ng' of the word 'bang'.
- The letter 'j' is pronounced like the 's' in 'treasure'.

Accents

- French vowels often have marks called accents above them, such as **é**, **à** or **î**. Vowels with accents are pronounced differently from vowels without accents.

- The letter 'c' sometimes has an accent underneath it, eg in the word '**ça**'. This letter 'c' should be pronounced like the 's' in 'sock', not like the 'c' in 'cat'.

Speaking to people

In French, there are two different words for 'you'. You use **tu** when you speak to a friend or an adult you know well. You use **vous** when you speak to more than one friend or an adult you do not know very well.

Masculine and feminine words

In French, some words are masculine and some are feminine. There are different words for 'the':

le salon   (masculine singular)
la porte   (feminine singular)

When the word begins with a vowel you use **l'**, eg **l'**église.

All plural words have the same word for 'the':

les salons (masculine plural)
les portes (feminine plural)

Meeting people

French people have different ways of greeting someone they meet. They use very polite greetings for people they do not know well and more friendly greetings for close friends.

Monsieur Flaubert meets a man he does not know very well.

> **Bonjour!**
> *(Bongjoor!)*
> Good morning!

> **Bonjour, Monsieur Flaubert.**
> *(Bongjoor, Mersyer Flowbair.)*
> Good morning, Mr Flaubert.

> **Comment allez-vous?**
> *(Commong tallay-voo?)*
> How are you?

> **Très bien, merci.**
> *(Tray beeyang, mairsee.)*
> Very well, thank you.

Marie and Jean meet their friends outside the shops.

> **Salut, ça va?**
> *(Salew, sah vah?)*
> Hello, how're you doing?

> **Ça va merci, et toi?**
> *(Sah vah mairsee, ay twah?)*
> Fine thank you, and you?

> **Au revoir.**
> *(Orvwahr.)*
> Goodbye.

> **A bientôt.**
> *(Ah beeyangtoh.)*
> See you soon.

Monsieur Flaubert welcomes visitors to his home for dinner.

Bonsoir!
(Bongswahr!)
Good evening!

The phrase 'Bonne nuit' is only used last thing at night.

Bonne nuit, maman.
(Bonn nwee, mamong.)
Good night, Mummy.

Bonne nuit, Jean.
(Bonn nwee, Jong.)
Good night, Jean.

When people meet, they often like to discuss the weather. You will find some phrases describing the weather on page 55.

'Bonjour' can also mean 'good afternoon' as well as 'good morning'.

BOUCHERIE

Bonjour, Madame. Il fait beau aujourd'hui, n'est-ce pas?
(Bongjoor, Madam. Eel fay boh ohjoordwee, nesspah?)
Good afternoon, madam. It's a fine day, isn't it?

Oui, il fait chaud.
(Wee, eel fay shoh.)
Yes, it is hot.

29

Making friends

The Flaubert family is at the beach for the day. Monsieur and Madame Flaubert are sunbathing with the rest of the family while Marie and Jean are busy making friends.

Bonjour, comment tu t'appelles?
(Bongjoor, commong tew tappell?)
Hello, what is your name?

Je m'appelle Edward, et toi?
(Jer mappell Edward, ay twah?)
My name is Edward, and yours?

Je m'appelle Marie. Quel âge as-tu?
(Jer mappell Marree. Kell ahj ah-tew?)
My name is Marie. How old are you?

J'ai dix ans.
(Jay deez ong.)
I am ten.

Tu habites où?
(Tew abbeet oo?)
Where do you live?

J'habite en Angleterre.
(Jabbeett onong-glertair.)
I live in England.

Marie and Edward introduce their brother and sister.

Voici mon frère Jean.
(Vwahsee mong frair Jong.)
This is my brother Jean.

Voici ma soeur Emily.
(Vwahsee mah serr Emily.)
This is my sister Emily.

Tu parles français?
(Tew pahrl frongssay?)
Do you speak French?

Pardon, je ne comprends pas.
(Pahrdong, jer ner comprong pah.)
Sorry, I do not understand.

The other members of the Flaubert family enjoy a restful afternoon.

la famille
(lah fammeeyer)
family

le père
(ler pair)
father

la grand-mère
(lah grong-mair)
grandmother

la mère
(lah mair)
mother

l'oncle
(longkler)
uncle

la tante
(lah tongt)
aunt

le grand-père
(ler grong-pair)
grandfather

31

Finding the way

Madame Flaubert and her children visit a town that they have not been to before.

Pardon Madame, y a t'il un café près d'ici?
(Pahrdong Madam, eeyateel ung kaffay pray deessee?)
Excuse me, is there a café near here?

Oui, Madame.
(Wee, Madam.)
Yes, madam.

C'est loin?
(Say lwang?)
Is it far?

Merci.
(Mairsee.)
Thank you.

C'est au coin de la rue.
(Say toh kwang der lah rew.)
It is on the corner of the street.

Je vous en prie.
(Jer voo zong pree.)
It is a pleasure.

Direction words

à gauche *(ah gohsh)* left	**derrière** *(derryair)* behind	**devant** *(dervong)* in front of	**à droite** *(ah drwaht)* right
à côté de *(ah kohtay der)* next to		**tout droit** *(too drwah)* straight on	**en face de** *(ong fass der)* opposite
jusqu'à *(jewsskah)* as far as	**près d'ici** *(pray deessee)* near here	**là-bas** *(lah-bah)* over there	**entre** *(ongtrer)* between

On their way to the station, Marie and Jean get lost.

Places to ask for

la gendarmerie
(lah jongdarmeree)
police station

l'hôpital
(lohpeetahl)
hospital

la cabine téléphonique
(lah kabbeen taylayfoneek)
telephone box

l'église
(laygleez)
church

les toilettes
(lay twahlett)
toilets

Staying in a hotel or house

Monsieur and Madame Flaubert are on holiday at a hotel. While they are away, Marie and Jean stay at their grandparents' house.

Je voudrais réserver une chambre.
(Jer voodray rayzairvay ewn shongbrer.)
I would like to book a room.

Oui, Monsieur. Que désirez-vous?
(Wee, Mersyer. Ker dayzeeray-voo?)
Yes, sir. What would you like?

Une chambre pour deux personnes.
(Ewn shongbrer poor der pairsonn.)
A double room.

Le dîner est à quelle heure?
(Ler deenay ay tah kell err?)
What time is dinner?

A huit heures, Madame.
(Ah weet err, Madam.)
At eight o'clock, madam.

Voici votre clef, Monsieur.
(Vwahsee vottrer klay, Mersyer.)
Here is your key, sir.

le porteur
(ler porterr)
porter

la valise
(lah valeez)
suitcase

l'ascenseur
(lassongserr)
lift

la clef
(lah klay)
key

le toit
(ler twah)
roof

la maison
(lah mayzong)
house

le grenier
(ler grernyay)
attic

la salle de bains
(lah sall der bang)
bathroom

la fenêtre
(lah fernettrer)
window

la chambre
(lah shongbrer)
bedroom

le lit
(ler lee)
bed

la douche
(lah doosh)
shower

le sol
(ler soll)
floor

l'armoire
(larmwahr)
wardrobe

le fauteuil
(ler fohter-yer)
armchair

le salon
(ler sallong)
living room

la porte
(lah port)
door

la télévision
(lah taylayveezyong)
television

la cuisine
(lah kweezeen)
kitchen

la salle à manger
(lah sallamongjay)
dining room

la chaise
(lah shehz)
chair

la table
(lah tahbler)
table

l'escalier
(leskalyay)
staircase

Camping

le matelas pneumatique
(ler matterlah pnermatteek)
lilo

le lit de camp
(ler lee der cong)
camp bed

l'eau
(loh)
water

le piquet
(ler peekay)
tent peg

Eau
Potable

(Oh pohtahbler)
Drinking water

le réchaud
(ler rayshoh)
stove

It is the summer holidays. The Flaubert family is staying at a campsite that provides its own tents which are very comfortable.

Où est-ce que je peux prendre une douche?
(Oo essker jer per prongdrer ewn doosh?)
Where can I take a shower?

Là-bas, je crois.
(Lah-bah, jer crwah.)
Over there, I think.

(Rayzairvay oh caravan)
Caravans only

Réservé
aux
Caravanes

le tapis de sol
(ler tappee der soll)
groundsheet

36

la tente
(lah tongt)
tent

la caravane
(lah caravan)
caravan

le maillet
(ler my-yay)
mallet

TOILETTES

(Twahlett)
Toilets

Je vais au magasin du camping.
(Jer vay zoh magazang dew congpeeng.)
I am going to the campsite shop.

Attends-moi!
(Attong-mwah!)
Wait for me!

le terrain de camping
(ler tairang der congpeeng)
campsite

la remorque
(lah rermork)
trailer

Parking Interdit

(Parkeeng angtairdee)
No parking

le camping gaz
(ler congpeeng gaz)
camping gas

le sac de couchage
(ler sack der cooshahj)
sleeping bag

Going shopping

The Flaubert family is out shopping. They visit the baker, the market and the newsagent.

The baker

Bonjour. Je voudrais deux pains, s'il vous plaît.
(Bongjoor. Jer voodray der pang, seelvooplay.)
Hello. I would like two loaves of bread, please.

Oui, bien sûr. C'est tout?
(Wee, beeyang sewr. Say too?)
Yes, certainly. Is that all?

Ça fait combien?
(Sah fay combeeyang?)
How much is that?

Ça fait sept francs cinquante, Madame.
(Sah fay sett frong sangkongt, Madam.)
That is seven francs fifty centimes, madam.

French money is divided into francs (F) and centimes (ct). There are 100 centimes in one franc. The numbers you will need to know for shopping are on page 55.

The market

Madame, vous désirez?
(Madam, voo dayzeeray?)
Can I help you, madam?

Un kilo de tomates, s'il vous plaît.
(Ung keeloh der tommaht, seelvooplay.)
A kilo of tomatoes, please.

les pommes
(lay pomm)
apples

les tomates
(lay tommaht)
tomatoes

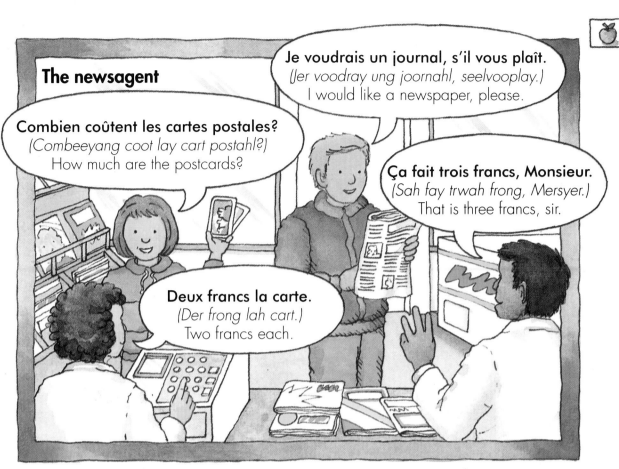

The newsagent

Je voudrais un journal, s'il vous plaît.
(Jer voodray ung joornahl, seelvooplay.)
I would like a newspaper, please.

Combien coûtent les cartes postales?
(Combeeyang coot lay cart postahl?)
How much are the postcards?

Ça fait trois francs, Monsieur.
(Sah fay trwah frong, Mersyer.)
That is three francs, sir.

Deux francs la carte.
(Der frong lah cart.)
Two francs each.

Shopping words

faire des courses	**je voudrais**	**je regarde seulement**	**acheter**
(fair day coorss)	*(jer voodray)*	*(jer rergard serlermong)*	*(ashtay)*
to go shopping	I would like	I am only looking	to buy

coûter	**un kilo**	**un litre**	**ouvert**	**soldes**
(cootay)	*(ung keeloh)*	*(ung leetrer)*	*(oovair)*	*(solld)*
to cost	a kilo	a litre	open	sale

une livre	**Combien coûte…?**	**libre service**
(ewn leevrer)	*(Combeeyang coot…?)*	*(leebrer sairveess)*
half a kilo	How much is…?	self-service

les poires	**les pommes de terre**	**les carottes**	**les choux**
(lay pwahr)	*(lay pomm der tair)*	*(lay carott)*	*(lay shoo)*
pears	potatoes	carrots	cabbages

The post office and bank

Marie and Edward visit the post office while Madame Flaubert is at the bank.

Combien coûte un timbre pour une carte postale pour l'Angleterre?
(Combeeyang coot ung tangbrer poor ewn cart postahl poor long-glertair?)
How much is a stamp for a postcard to England?

Deux francs.
(Der frong.)
Two francs.

Je voudrais quatre timbres, s'il vous plaît.
(Jer voodray kahtrer tangbrer, seelvooplay.)
I would like four stamps, please.

Oui, bien sûr.
(Wee, beeyang sewr.)
Yes, certainly.

Où se trouve la boîte aux lettres?
(Oo ser troov lah bwaht oh lettrer?)
Where is the post box?

Là-bas.
(Lah-bah.)
Over there.

POSTES

la lettre
(lah lettrer)
letter

le timbre
(ler tangbrer)
stamp

la télécopie
(lah taylaycoppee)
fax

la télécarte
(lah taylaycart)
telephone card

Pourriez-vous me donner de la monnaie?
(Pooreeay-voo mer donnay der lah monnay?)
Could I have some small change?

Puis-je changer un chèque de voyage ici?
(Pwee-jer shongjay ung sheck der vwah-yahj eessee?)
Can I cash a traveller's cheque here?

le billet
(ler beeyay)
bank note

la pièce
(lah pyess)
coin

le chèque de voyage
(ler sheck der vwah-yahj)
traveller's cheque

la monnaie
(lah monnay)
small change

41

Eating out

French people enjoy going out with friends and family for a drink or a meal.

Madame Flaubert meets a friend at a café.

> **Deux cafés, s'il vous plaît.**
> *(Der kaffay, seelvooplay.)*
> Two coffees, please.

> **Bien sûr, Madame.**
> *(Beeyang sewr, Madam.)*
> Certainly, madam.

The Flaubert family visits the countryside and enjoys a picnic in the sunshine.

> **Je voudrais une tranche de quiche.**
> *(Jer voodray ewn trangsh der keesh.)*
> I would like a slice of quiche.

> **Sers-toi.**
> *(Sair-twah.)*
> Help yourself.

le pique-nique
(ler peek-neek)
picnic

> **J'ai faim.**
> *(Jay fang.)*
> I am hungry.

> **Veux-tu un sandwich au jambon?**
> *(Ver-too ung songdweech oh jangbong?)*
> Would you like a ham sandwich?

It is Madame Flaubert's birthday. She and Monsieur Flaubert dine at a restaurant.

Bon appétit!
(Bonn appaytee!)
Enjoy your meal!

C'est bon?
(Say bong?)
Is it good?

C'est délicieux.
(Say dayleessyer.)
It is delicious.

Voulez-vous autre chose.
(Voolay-voo zohtrer shohz?)
Would you like anything else?

Non. L'addition, s'il vous plaît.
(Nong. Laddeesseeong, seelvooplay.)
No. The bill, please.

Useful words for eating out

Madame *(Madam)* waitress	**le menu** *(ler mernew)* menu	**la serviette** *(lah sairveeyett)* napkin	**l'addition** *(laddeessyong)* bill	**Monsieur** *(Mersyer)* waiter
la nappe *(lah napp)* tablecloth	**le couteau** *(ler kootoh)* knife	**la fourchette** *(lah foorshett)* fork	**la cuillère** *(lah kweeyair)* spoon	**le verre** *(ler vair)* glass

Visiting places

Monsieur and Madame Flaubert like to take their children to the cinema and other places of entertainment.

Madame Flaubert takes Jean and Pierre to see a cartoon film.

J'adore les dessins animés.
(Jaddor lay dessang zannimay.)
I love cartoons.

Quel est le prix des places?
(Kell ay ler pree day plass?)
How much are the tickets?

Moi aussi.
(Mwah ohssee.)
Me too.

The Flaubert family often visits the tourist information centre.
It has leaflets that show interesting places to visit.

le centre de loisir
(ler songtrer der lwahzeer)
leisure centre

les grottes
(lay grott)
caves

le théâtre
(ler tayahtrer)
theatre

le château
(ler shattoh)
castle

44

The Flaubert family visits a sound and light show at a château. The show is called a 'son et lumière' *(sonnay lewmeeair)*. It tells the history of the château.

C'est très joli.
(Say tray jollee.)
It is very pretty.

Je suis fatigué.
(Jer swee fateegay.)
I am tired.

C'est intéressant, n'est-ce pas?
(Say tangtairessang, nesspah?)
It is interesting, isn't it?.

le cirque
(ler seerk)
circus

la réserve nationale
(lah raysairv nassyonal)
nature reserve

le musée
(ler mewzay)
museum

45

Games and sports

le rugby
(ler rergbee)
rugby

le golf
(ler golf)
golf

le football
(ler footbohll)
football

le ski
(ler skee)
skiing

la planche à voile
(lah plongsh ah vwahl)
windsurfing

l'aviron
(laveerong)
rowing

le ski nautique
(ler skee nohteek)
water skiing

**Marie and Jean like to play
different games and sports.**

la balançoire
(lah ballongswahr)
swing

C'est à toi.
(Say tah twah.)
Your turn.

Est-ce que je peux jouer?
(Essker jer per jooay?)
Can I play?

les billes
(lay beeyer)
marbles

l'équitation
(laykitassyong)
riding

le patinage
(ler patteenahj)
skating

faire du jogging
(fair dew jogging)
to go jogging

le badminton
(ler badmeengtong)
badminton

la natation
(lah nahtassyong)
swimming

Attrape!
(Attrapp!)
Catch!

cache-cache
(cash-cash)
hide and seek

...Quatre, cinq, six...
(...Kahtrer, sangk, seess...)
...Four, five, six...

la pêche
(lah pesh)
fishing

le tennis
(ler tenneess)
tennis

les boules
(lay booll)
bowls

la gymnastique
(lah jimnasteek)
gymnastics

le volleyball
(ler volleebohll)
volleyball

le cyclisme
(ler seekleezm)
cycling

Accidents and illnesses

In France, there are different telephone numbers for the police, the fire brigade and the ambulance service.

On m'a volé mon sac à main!
(Ong mah vollay mong sak ah mang!)
My handbag has been stolen.

Au feu!
(Oh fer!)
Fire!

Au secours!
(Oh sercoor!)
Help!

Venez vite!
(Vernay veet!)
Come quickly!

Accident words

l'agent de police
(lahjong der pohleess)
policeman

le pompier
(ler pongpyay)
fireman

l'ambulancier
(longbewlongssyay)
ambulance man

la voiture de police
(lah vwahtewr der pohleess)
police car

la voiture de pompiers
(lah vwahtewr der pongpyay)
fire engine

l'ambulance
(longbewlongss)
ambulance

Je me suis fait piquer par une guêpe.
(Jer mer swee fay peekay parr ewn gep.)
I have been stung by a wasp.

J'ai attrapé un coup de soleil.
(Jay attrappay ung coo der sohlay.)
I am sunburnt.

l'aspirine
(laspeereen)
aspirin

le médecin
(ler medsang)
doctor

l'infirmière
(langfermeeair)
nurse

le pansement
(ler pongsmong)
sticking plaster

J'ai mal à la tête.
(Jay mal ah lah tett.)
I have a headache.

Tu as de la fièvre.
(Tew ah der lah feeyairvrer.)
You have a temperature.

Je suis enrhumée.
(Jer swee zongrewmay.)
I have a cold.

J'ai mal au ventre.
(Jay mal oh vongtrer.)
I have a stomach ache.

Travelling

The Flaubert family travels by different kinds of transport.

Nous sommes en panne.
(Noo somm zong pann.)
We have broken down.

Où est le garage le plus proche?
(Oo ay ler garahj ler ploo prosh?)
Where is the nearest garage?

la voiture
(lah vwahtewr)
car

Un billet pour Paris.
(Ung beeyay poor Parree.)
A ticket to Paris.

Railway words

la gare	**le billet**	**l'horaire**
(lah garr)	*(ler beeyay)*	*(lorrair)*
station	ticket	timetable

le quai	**le guichet**
(ler kay)	*(ler geeshay)*
platform	ticket office

le composteur	**le bagage**	**la voiture-buffet**
(ler congposterr)	*(ler bagahj)*	*(lah vwahtewr-bewfay)*
ticket puncher	luggage	buffet car

la guarde	**le chariot à bagages**
(lah gard)	*(ler sharreeoh ah bagahj)*
guard	trolley

More useful words

Time

Quelle heure est-il, s'il te plaît?
(Kell err ayteel, seelterplay?)
What time is it?

Il est trois heures.
(Eel ay trwah zerr.)
It is three o'clock.

Il est trois heures dix.
(Eel ay trwah zerr deess.)
It is ten past three.

Il est trois heures et quart.
(Eel ay trwah zerr ay kahr.)
It is quarter past three.

Il est trois heures et demie.
(Eel ay trwah zerr ay dermee.)
It is half past three.

Il est quatre heures moins le quart.
(Eel ay kahtrer err mwang ler kahr.)
It is quarter to four.

Il est quatre heures moins dix.
(Eel ay kahtrer err mwang deess.)
It is ten minutes to four.

Il est midi.
(Eel ay meedee.)
It is midday.

Il est minuit.
(Eel ay meenwee.)
It is midnight.

Times of the day

l'après-midi
(lappray-meedee)
afternoon

la nuit
(lah nwee)
night

le matin
(ler mattang)
morning

le soir
(ler swahr)
evening

janvier
(jongveeay)
January

février
(fayvreeay)
February

mars
(mahrss)
March

avril
(avreel)
April

mai
(may)
May

juin
(jwang)
June

The months of the year and days of the week

The French do not use capital letters at the beginning of words for months of the year or days of the week.

lundi	**mardi**	**mercredi**
(lerngdee)	*(mahrdee)*	*(maircrerdee)*
Monday	Tuesday	Wednesday

jeudi	**vendredi**
(jerdee)	*(vongdrerdee)*
Thursday	Friday

samedi	**dimanche**
(sammdee)	*(deemongsh)*
Saturday	Sunday

The seasons

le printemps
(ler prangtong)
spring

l'été
(laytay)
summer

l'automne
(lohton)
autumn

l'hiver
(leevair)
winter

juillet
(jweeay)
July

août
(oott)
August

septembre
(sayptongbrer)
September

octobre
(oktohbrer)
October

novembre
(nohvongbrer)
November

décembre
(dayssongbrer)
December

Clothes and parts of the body

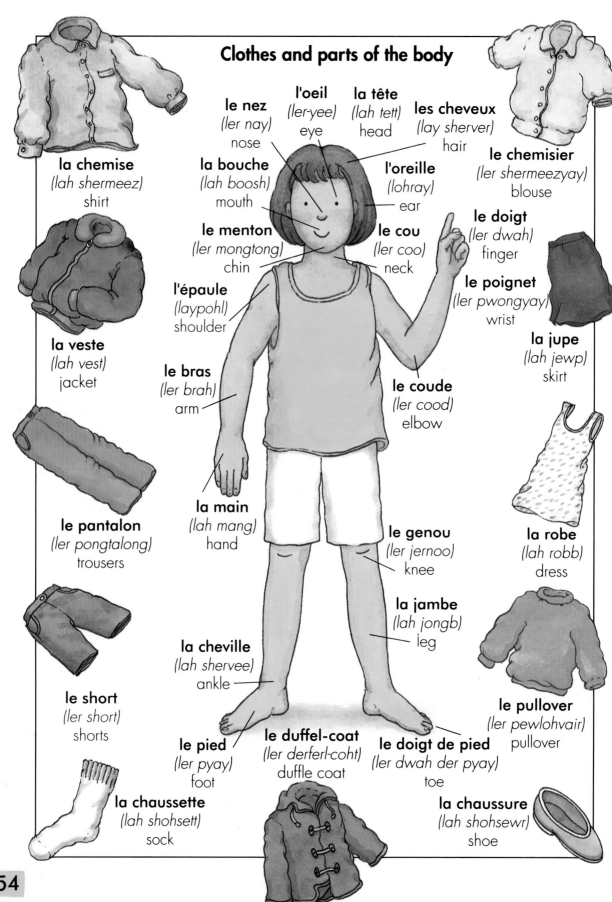

la chemise
(lah shermeez)
shirt

le nez
(ler nay)
nose

l'oeil
(ler-yee)
eye

la tête
(lah tett)
head

les cheveux
(lay sherver)
hair

le chemisier
(ler shermeezyay)
blouse

la bouche
(lah boosh)
mouth

l'oreille
(lohray)
ear

le doigt
(ler dwah)
finger

le menton
(ler mongtong)
chin

le cou
(ler coo)
neck

le poignet
(ler pwongyay)
wrist

l'épaule
(laypohl)
shoulder

la veste
(lah vest)
jacket

le bras
(ler brah)
arm

le coude
(ler cood)
elbow

la jupe
(lah jewp)
skirt

la main
(lah mang)
hand

le pantalon
(ler pongtalong)
trousers

le genou
(ler jernoo)
knee

la robe
(lah robb)
dress

la jambe
(lah jongb)
leg

la cheville
(lah shervee)
ankle

le short
(ler short)
shorts

le pied
(ler pyay)
foot

le duffel-coat
(ler derferl-coht)
duffle coat

le doigt de pied
(ler dwah der pyay)
toe

le pullover
(ler pewlohvair)
pullover

la chaussette
(lah shohsett)
sock

la chaussure
(lah shohsewr)
shoe

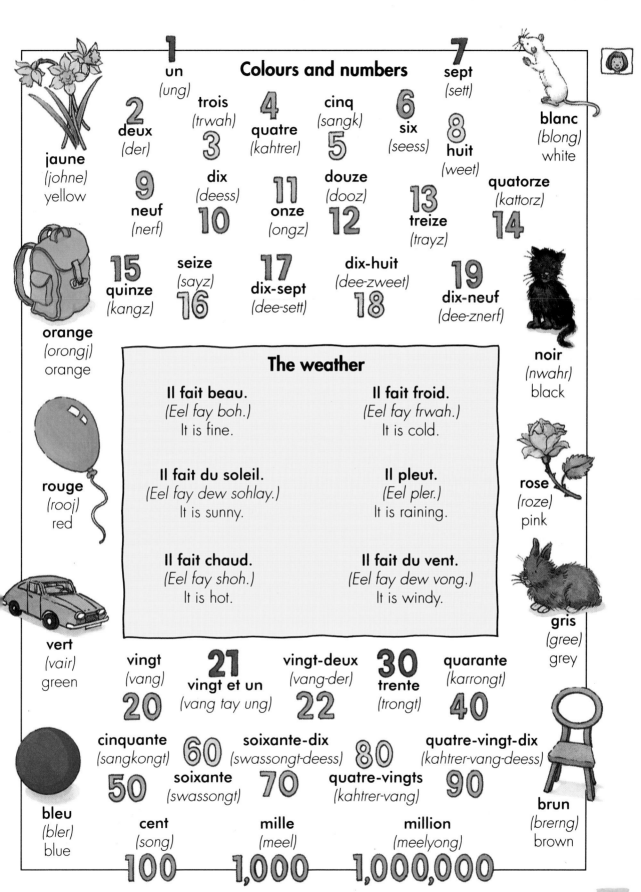

Colours and numbers

1 un *(ung)*

2 deux *(der)*

trois *(trwah)* **3**

4 quatre *(kahtrer)*

cinq *(sangk)* **5**

6 **six** *(seess)*

8 huit *(weet)*

7 sept *(sett)*

blanc *(blong)* white

9 **neuf** *(nerf)*

dix *(deess)* **10**

11 onze *(ongz)*

douze *(dooz)* **12**

13 treize *(trayz)*

quatorze *(kattorz)* **14**

15 quinze *(kangz)*

seize *(sayz)* **16**

17 dix-sept *(dee-sett)*

dix-huit *(dee-zweet)* **18**

19 dix-neuf *(dee-znerf)*

jaune *(johne)* yellow

orange *(orongj)* orange

rouge *(rooj)* red

noir *(nwahr)* black

rose *(roze)* pink

The weather

Il fait beau.
(Eel fay boh.)
It is fine.

Il fait froid.
(Eel fay frwah.)
It is cold.

Il fait du soleil.
(Eel fay dew sohlay.)
It is sunny.

Il pleut.
(Eel pler.)
It is raining.

Il fait chaud.
(Eel fay shoh.)
It is hot.

Il fait du vent.
(Eel fay dew vong.)
It is windy.

gris *(gree)* grey

vert *(vair)* green

vingt *(vang)* **20**

21 vingt et un *(vang tay ung)*

vingt-deux *(vang-der)* **22**

30 trente *(trongt)*

quarante *(karrongt)* **40**

cinquante *(sangkongt)* **50**

60 soixante *(swassongt)*

soixante-dix *(swassongt-deess)* **70**

80 quatre-vingts *(kahtrer-vang)*

quatre-vingt-dix *(kahtrer-vang-deess)* **90**

bleu *(bler)* blue

brun *(brerng)* brown

cent *(song)* **100**

mille *(meel)* **1,000**

million *(meelyong)* **1,000,000**

Animals

le crocodile
(ler crocohdeel)
crocodile

la baleine
(lah bahlenn)
whale

l'ours
(loorss)
bear

le loup
(ler loo)
wolf

le dauphin
(ler dohfang)
dolphin

le panda
(ler pongda)
panda

le zèbre
(ler zebrer)
zebra

le tigre
(ler teegrer)
tiger

le gorille
(ler goreeyer)
gorilla

le lion
(ler leeong)
lion

Index

le kangourou
(ler kongooroo)
kangaroo

l'éléphant
(laylayfong)
elephant

la girafe
(lah jeeraff)
giraffe